How To Use This

READ TOGETHER • DO TOGETHER™ BOOK

This is a very special book. Why? Because it's all about YOU!

Since it's your story, you can write or draw in the empty white boxes in the book. (A grown-up can help if you want.)

And don't worry if something doesn't turn out quite perfectly... that's what makes it special!

Read, draw, talk, laugh and have fun!

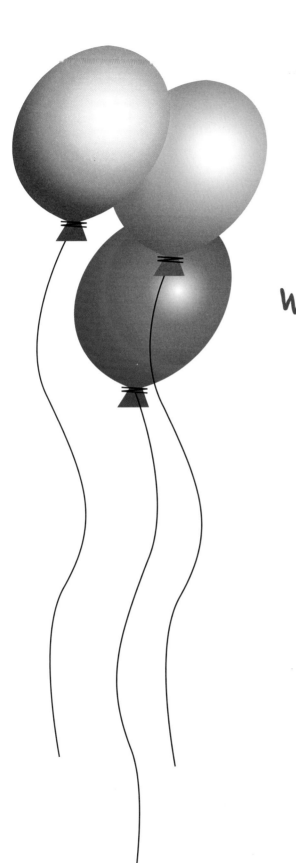

With love to Halia and Kylie
~ Mimi

Lucky to Live
in
South Carolina

By Kate B. Jerome

Illustrations by Roger Radtke

ARCADIA KIDS

South Carolina is home—and I think quite a lot
that I'm lucky to live in this wonderful spot.
Why is it special? That's easy to see.
It's the place that begins the whole story of me!

A picture of me

by

You

Age

South Carolina roots keep me strong and it's really quite **neat** that the place they begin is my very own street.

Where I live

It's close to

South Carolina is in the southeast part of the United States.

Southern charm is quite **famous** as everyone knows and the way that I speak is one way that it shows.

My Southern charm is hard to beat!

How interesting! The state butterfly of South Carolina is the Eastern Tiger Swallowtail.

Good Friends!

is my favorite thing to do.

South Carolina **cooks** are so skilled they can please any guest.
(No surprise that they think homemade food is the **best**.)

Fresh Peach Pie

Frogmore Stew

I love to eat

I didn't think I would like

...but I do!

Frogmore Stew can also be called "Lowcountry Boil" or "Beaufort Stew."

Taking trips to the **park** makes me want to see more.
I have quite a long list of fun things to **explore**.

South Carolina Trip List

• Riverbanks Zoo and Botanical Gardens
• South Carolina Aquarium
• Jocassee Gorges

It was fun to visit

Next up:

Can't wait to start packing!

In this state we make **noise** for our favorite home teams.
Win or lose—all great plays deserve very loud **screams**.

My Team

Go ahead! Color the T-shirt in your team colors!

South Carolina land provides homes for more **critters** than me.
So it's good to **protect** even what we can't see.

Some of my favorite animals:

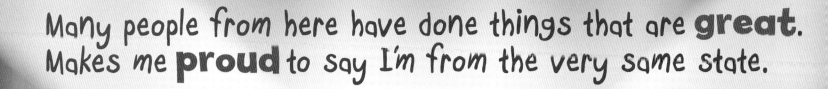

Many people from here have done things that are **great**.
Makes me **proud** to say I'm from the very same state.

CHARLES PINCKNEY
Governor and Signer of Constitution
(Charleston)

ALTHEA GIBSON
Major title-winning tennis champion
(Silver)

CHARLES H. TOWNES
Nobel Prize-winning physicist
(Greenville)

ANDIE MCDOWELL
Model and actress
(Gaffney)

SOUTH CAROLINA BORN

CONGRATULATIONS TO MY HERO

I think

is great because

And guess what? You don't have to be famous to be a hero!

In South Carolina good **music** will send out a beat that will start in your ears but end up in your **feet!**

Songs I like to sing:

Darius Rucker, the Grammy-winning singer, was born in Charleston, SC.

South Carolina people take pride in the things they **create**.
Bright ideas **shine** through from all over the state.

I'm pretty good at making

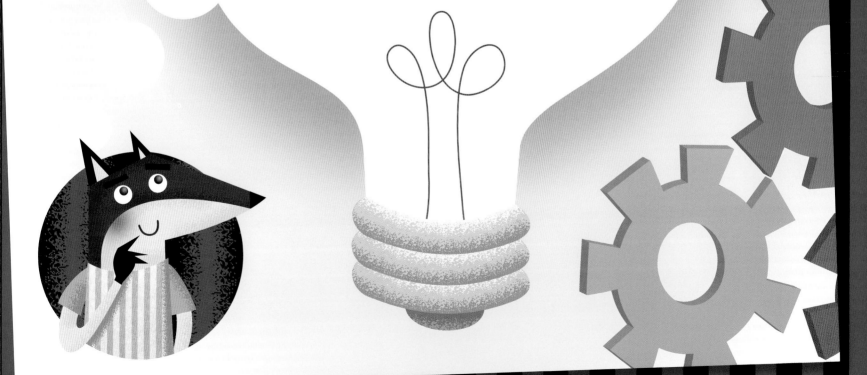

In this state **celebrations** are always great fun.
People **laughing** and sharing is just how it's done.

South Carolina became a state on May 23, 1788!

My favorite celebration is

because

As my own **story** grows I will never forget
all the places I've been and the **people** I've met.
Yes, the **memories** I have of this wonderful place
are the ones that will always bring **smiles** to my face.

When I grow up I'd like to

Keep exploring! Keep learning! Keep growing!

My Family Tree

Me

South Carolina Roots!

A tracing of my hand

My Time Capsule

Things you need:
- a cardboard box (big enough to fit this book and some other small things)
- one blank piece of paper and an envelope
- three index cards
- some favorite little "stuff" (like pictures, artwork, something that shows your favorite team on it)
- a recent newspaper
- tape and some ribbon

First: Fill out two of the index cards. On one, describe your perfect day. On the other, list the price of some things you often use or do.

My perfect day is when...

Milk costs
_____

A Movie ticket costs
_____

Next: Use the blank piece of paper to write a letter to your future self! When you are done, put it in the envelope and seal it shut.

Dear Future Me,
When I think about you in the future
I wonder...

Then: Put the index cards, this book, the letter to your future self and the other special "stuff" in the box. Wrap it like a present with the newspaper. Put ribbon around it. Then write on the last index card: DO NOT OPEN FOR 10 YEARS! and tape it to the box.

Finally: Put the box in the back of a closet or somewhere where you won't see it too much. Then wait ten years... and OPEN!

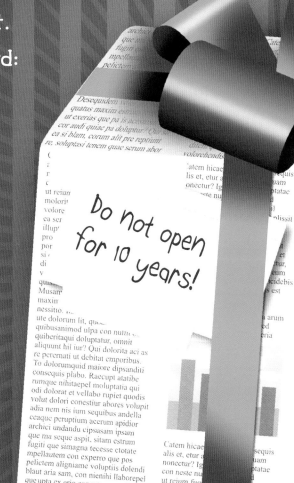

The countdown is starting!

Written by Kate B. Jerome
Illustrations by Roger Radtke
Design and Production: Lumina Datamatics, Inc.
Research: Lisa A. Boehm

Published by Arcadia Kids, a division of Arcadia Publishing and
The History Press, Charleston, SC

For all general information contact Arcadia Publishing at:
Telephone: 843-853-2070
Email: sales@arcadiapublishing.com

For Customer Service and Orders:
Toll Free: 1-888-313-2665
Visit us on the internet at
www.arcadiapublishing.com

Library of Congress Cataloging-in-Publication data is
on file with the publisher.

Printed in China

ARCADIA KIDS